Citrus Creatures

Make Your Own

Iryna Stepanova

Sergiy Kabachenko

FIREFLY BOOKS

Contents

Introduction

Citrus fruits come in many varieties. The most popular citrus is the orange. Over the course of one year, people eat more oranges than apples globally. The orange is a popular dessert fruit and contains the daily recommended amount of vitamin C. Mandarins are very similar to oranges. An orange is bigger than a mandarin, but the mandarin peel and segments separate more easily. Pomegranate seeds are available ready to serve, saving you from the messy task of working with the whole fruit.

The lime and lemon are not considered dessert fruits. Lemon is served with tea in many countries (although not in China, which has the largest tea-drinking population in the world). Lemons are mainly used to improve the taste of fruit and vegetable salads, and in cooking and baking. The lime is a hybrid citrus. Native to Southeast Asia, its apparent path of introduction was through the Middle East to North Africa, then to Sicily and Andalusia and via Spanish explorers to the West Indies. From the Caribbean, lime cultivation spread to tropical and subtropical North America, including Mexico, Florida (notably in the Florida Keys), and later, California.

Grapefruits have a slightly bitter taste, but are nonetheless considered a dessert fruit. The kumquat is a close relative of the citrus family. Citrus fruits are often used in various weight-loss and health-improvement diets.

We will be using citrus fruits to make amusing figures and shapes to decorate your festive table and make an indelible impression on your visitors, both children and adults alike.

So, let's begin. Arm yourself with the necessary tools, as well as a good dose of patience and humor, and success will be yours. Enjoy!

Elephant

INGREDIENTS

1 mandarin
1 orange
4 red grapes
1 blueberry

1 Use the mandarin for the head. Cut out an ear from the peel.

2 Separate the ear and bend it as shown.

3 Cut out a second ear in the same way.

4 Cut out a strip of peel for the trunk.

5 Separate it from the mandarin.

6 Cut two semicircles for the eyelids.

7 Cut a blueberry in half.

8 Cut one half into quarters. These are the eyes.

9 Put the eyes under the eyelids.

10 Cut the tip from a red grape.

11 Place the tip cut side down. It is a leg. Make four legs in all.

12 Place half of the orange on the legs. This is the body. Place the head next to the body.

13 You can also place the head on top of the body.

Lion

INGREDIENTS

2 oranges
1 red grape
1 green grape
1 blue grape
1 blueberry
2 pomegranate seeds

1 Cut one orange into round slices.

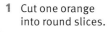

2 Select the biggest slices. Make an incision in the center. Separate all of the segments.

3 Cut out triangular segments from the peel.

4 Bend the peel in the form of a mane.

5 Place a round slice on top. This is the head.

6 Peel the second orange and separate into segments.

7 Place two segments on the head. These are the cheeks. Put one more segment between the cheeks for the nose.

8 Cut off the tip from a red grape. This is an ear.

9 Cut another tip for the second ear. Place the ears on the mane.

10 Cut a green grape in half. These are the eyes. Cut out notches to hold the pupils.

11 Cut off two round edge slices from a blueberry. These are the pupils.

12 Place the pupils on the eyes. Place the eyes on the head. Use two pomegranate seeds for the mouth. Use half of the blue grape for the nose.

13 Place one orange segment against the head. This is the body. Cut out strips of peel for the legs and tail.

Monkey

INGREDIENTS

2 oranges
3 round slices of lime
1 red grape
1 green grape
1 blueberry
6 blackberries

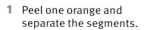
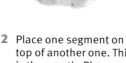

1 Peel one orange and separate the segments.

2 Place one segment on top of another one. This is the mouth. Place a third segment on top. This is the head.

3 Cut the green grape in half. These are the eyes. Use two blueberry halves for the pupils.

4 Place the pupils on the eyes. Place the eyes on the head.

5 Cut off a slice from the red grape. This is the nose.

6 Use two slices of lime for the ears. Place the nose and ears on the head.

7 Lay out the hair using the blackberries.

8 Cut the second orange in half. One half is the body.

9 Cut a round slice from the second half. Cut the slice in half.

10 Place one semicircle under the head. These are the shoulders.

11 Place two orange segments under the body. These are the legs. Use semicircles of lime for the feet.

12 Cut off a strip of peel from a round slice of orange.

13 This is the tail. Cut off one more strip for the arms.

Tiger

INGREDIENTS

1 orange
1 mandarin
2 red grapes
1 green grape
1 strawberry
2 blueberries
2 pomegranate seeds

1 Stand the orange on its base. Cut off a side slice and then four more slices. The remaining part of the orange is the head.

2 Peel the mandarin and separate all of the segments.

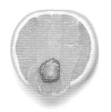

3 Place one segment of mandarin on the head. This is the chin. Use a round slice of strawberry for the mouth.

4 Cut off a tip from a red grape. This is the nose. Cut two round slices from the grape. These are the eyes.

5 Place the eyes on the head. Use two mandarin segments for the cheeks.

6 Use two blueberries for the pupils. Place the nose between the cheeks.

7 Lay out the body using round slices of orange.

8 Cut a strip of peel for the tail.

9 Place the head on the body.

10 Cut the green grape in half. These are the ears.

11 Attach the ears to the head.

12 Cut the whole red grape in half.

13 Cut each half into quarters.

14 Lay out legs using the quarters. Use pomegranate seeds for the paws.

Hamster

1 Place the orange on its base. Cut off a side slice. This is a cheek.

2 Cut off four more slices.

3 Place the medium-sized slice on the largest slice. Place a smaller slice on top. This is the head.

4 Cut a red grape in half. These are the ears.

5 Place the ears under the head.

6 Cut off the second cheek from the remaining piece of orange.

7 Use half of a red grape for the nose.

8 Place the cheek on the head. Place the nose between.

9 Cut the green grape in half. These are the eyes.

10 Cut a blueberry in half. These are the pupils.

11 Place the pupils on the eyes. Place the eyes on the head.

12 Cut one round slice of orange into semicircles. These are the arms and legs.

13 Place another round slice of orange on top. This is the body.

Bird

INGREDIENTS

1 orange

1 red grape

3 green grapes

1 blueberry

pomegranate seeds

1 Place the orange on its base. Cut off a side slice. This is the head.

2 Cut off four more slices.

3 Cut one big slice in half. One half is the top part of the beak. Cut off a segment from a smaller slice. This is the lower part of the beak.

4 Place the beak on the head.

5 Cut the red grape in half. These are the ears.

6 Cut off two round slices from a green grape.

7 Cut a blueberry in half. These are the pupils.

8 Place the green grape slices on the eyes. Place the pupils on top.

9 Place the eyes on the head. Lay the remaining section against the head. This is the neck.

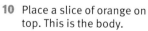

10 Place a slice of orange on top. This is the body.

11 Cut two green grapes in half.

12 Lay out a tail using three halves. Use a semicircle of orange for the wing.

13 Lay out legs and fingers using pomegranate seeds.

Cat

INGREDIENTS

1 orange

1 green grape

1 blueberry

1 strawberry

1 Stand the orange on its base. Cut off a thin outer slice. Cut off four more slices.

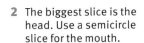

2 The biggest slice is the head. Use a semicircle slice for the mouth.

3 Cut the green grape in half. Cut one half into quarters. These are the ears.

4 Place the ears under the head.

5 Cut off one more side slice of the same size as the first cut side slice. These are for the under-eye area.

6 Place the under-eye pieces cut side up on the head. Use half of the strawberry for the nose.

7 Cut off two rounds from the green grape. These are the eyes.

8 Cut a blueberry in half. These are the pupils.

9 Place the pupils on the eyes. Place the eyes on the under-eye pieces.

10 Use a semicircle slice of orange for the body.

11 Cut off two strips from a round slice of orange. These are the legs. One of the side sections is the tail.

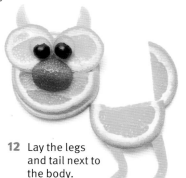

12 Lay the legs and tail next to the body.

13 You can also make a mouse from a semicircle of orange.

Giraffe

INGREDIENTS

1 orange

2 red grapes

1 green grape

1 blueberry

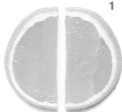

1 Cut the orange into round slices. Cut one round in half. These are the ears.

2 Cut off two strips from another round. These are the horns. The remaining sections are the legs.

3 Place the horns against the ears.

4 Arrange large and small rounds on top. This is the head.

5 Use a medium-sized round for the muzzle.

6 Use two round slices of green grape for the eyes. Use blueberry halves for the pupils. Place the pupils on the eyes.

7 Cut off two rounds from a red grape. These are the nostrils.

8 Place the eyes on the head. Place the nostrils on the muzzle.

9 Cut off four segments from the largest slice of orange.

10 Arrange the neck using the segments.

11 Place one round against the neck. This is the body. Place a strip of peel under the body. This is the tail. Place the legs next the body.

12 Cut half of a red grape in two. These are the hooves.

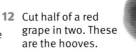

13 Place the hooves against the legs.

Bee

INGREDIENTS

2 round slices of orange
2 blueberries
2 round slices of lime
5 mandarin segments
cherry stems

1 One orange slice is the head.

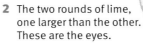

2 The two rounds of lime, one larger than the other. These are the eyes.

3 Place the eyes on the head. Use two blueberries for the pupils.

4 Cut off two large segments from one round of orange. These are the wings. Cut off two narrow segments.

5 One of the narrow segments is the proboscis. Place it on the head. Lay out a body using the mandarin segments.

6 Lay the wings against the body.

7 Use the cherry stems for the legs.

Fish

INGREDIENTS

1 orange

1 red grape

1 green grape

1 blueberry

1 round slice of lime

1 Cut the orange into round slices.

2 Cut one slice in half. One half is the head.

3 Cut off two rounds from the green grape. These are the eyes.

4 Cut a blueberry in half. These are the pupils.

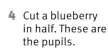

5 Place the pupils on the eyes. Place the eyes on the head.

6 Cut one red grape in lengthwise quarters.

7 Lay out a mouth using two of the quarters.

8 Lay out a body from orange slices.

9 Place a semicircle slice of orange against the body. This is the tail.

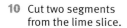

10 Cut two segments from the lime slice.

11 These are the fins.

Hedgehog

INGREDIENTS

1 round slice of orange
1 mandarin
2 green grapes
1 red grape
1 strawberry
1 blueberry
2 pomegranate seeds

1 Cut the orange slice in half.

2 One of the halves is the head.

3 Cut off the tips from a green grape. Cut the remaining middle piece in half, without fully severing. These are the eyes.

4 Cut the blueberry in half. These are the pupils.

5 Place the pupils on the eyes. Place the eyes on the head.

6 One half of the red grape is the nose. Use two pomegranate seeds for the mouth.

7 Peel the mandarin and separate it into segments.

8 Lay out the body using three segments.

9 Place five segments on top. This is the lower line of quills.

10 Lay out one more line of quills on top.

11 Cut off a tip from the second green grape. This is the stem of a mushroom.

12 Cut off the end of the strawberry. This is the mushroom cap.

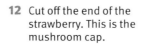

Bear

INGREDIENTS

1 orange

1 mandarin

1 red grape

1 green grape

1 blue grape

1 cherry

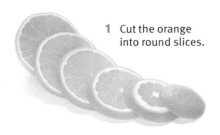

1 Cut the orange into round slices.

2 Place a small round on the largest round. This is the head. Place the outside slice on the head. This is the muzzle.

3 Peel the mandarin and separate it into segments.

4 Two segments are the ears.

5 Cut the red grape in half. These are the eyes.

6 Cut two rounds from the blue grape. These are the pupils.

7 Place two round slices of green grape on the eyes.

8 Place the pupils on top.

9 Place the eyes on the head. Place the cherry on the muzzle. This is the nose.

10 Use one round of orange for the body. Use the mandarin segments for the paws.

Owl

INGREDIENTS

2 oranges
1 lime
1 red grape
2 blueberries
1 strawberry

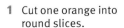

1 Cut one orange into round slices.

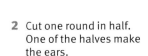

2 Cut one round in half. One of the halves make the ears.

3 Place another round on top. This is the head.

4 Cut off two rounds of lime for the rims of the eyes.

5 Place the rims on the head.

6 Cut the pointed end from the strawberry.

7 Place the strawberry on the head. This is the beak. Place two blueberries on the rims. These are the eyes.

8 Lay the remaining part of the lime next to the head. This is the body. Use a semicircle of orange for the tail.

9 Peel the second whole orange and separate it into segments.

10 Lay out six segments in the form of wings.

11 Cut a red grape in half. Cut out the feet as shown.

12 Place the feet on top of the tail.

Lobster

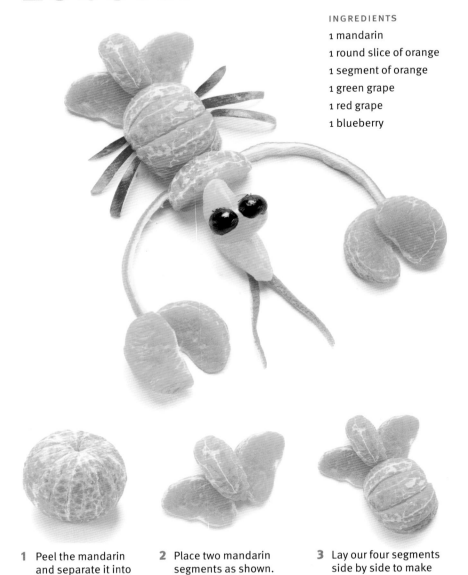

INGREDIENTS

1 mandarin
1 round slice of orange
1 segment of orange
1 green grape
1 red grape
1 blueberry

1   Peel the mandarin and separate it into segments.

2   Place two mandarin segments as shown. Place one more segment between them. This is the tail.

3   Lay our four segments side by side to make the body.

4 Cut half of the red grape into six strips.

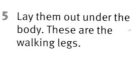

5 Lay them out under the body. These are the walking legs.

6 Cut the round slice of orange in half. Cut off two strips of the peel. These are the claws.

7 Lay the claws next to the body.

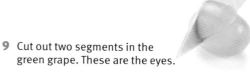

8 Lay a mandarin segment on top of the claws. Lay another segment to make the head.

9 Cut out two segments in the green grape. These are the eyes.

10 Cut off two slices from the opposite side for the pupils.

11 Cut a blueberry in half. These are the pupils.

12 Place the eyes on the head. Lay the pupils on the eyes.

13 Lay out claws from the mandarin segments. Use strips of the peel for the antennae.

Snail

INGREDIENTS

1 mandarin

2 round slices of orange

2 green grapes

2 red grapes

1 blue grape

1 Use one round orange slice for the head.

2 Cut off two rounds from the blue grape. These are the pupils.

3 Cut off outside slices from a green grape.

4 Cut one slice in half. These are the eyelids.

5 Cut the remaining middle part of the green grape in two. These are the eyes.

6 Place the eyes on the head and the eyelids on top. Place the pupils under the eyelids.

7 Cut a slice from a red grape.

8 Cut the slice in two. This is the mouth. Use a green grape for the nose.

9 Cut out two strips from an orange slice. These are the horns.

10 Cut off the tips from a red grape.

11 Place the tips on the horns. Place the horns under the head. Use a semicircle of orange for the body.

12 Peel a mandarin.

13 Separate one half of the mandarin and place it on top of the body. This is the shell.

Man

INGREDIENTS

2 mandarins
1 round slice of orange
1 segment of orange
1 slice of grapefruit
1 green grape
2 red grapes
1 blue grape
3 gooseberries or
  cherry tomatoes
2 pomegranate seeds

1 Cut out some mandarin peel in the form of a crescent. This is the mouth.

2 Cut the round slice of orange in half. Separate the peel from both sides.

3 Cut one strip of peel into pieces. These are the teeth.

4 Insert the teeth into the mouth. Use a whole mandarin for the head.

5 Use two gooseberries for the ears. Use the orange segment as a base for the eyes.

6 Cut off outer edge slices from the green grape.

7 Cut one slice in half. These are the eyelids.

8 Cut the remaining middle piece of grape in two. These are the eyes.

9 Cut off two round slices from the blue grape. These are the pupils.

10 Place the pupils on the eyes. Place the eyelids on top. Lay the eyes on the head.

11 Cut a round edge slice from the grapefruit. Cut out a crescent. This is the preform for the moustache.

12 Cut narrow strips along the lower edge of the preform to complete the moustache.

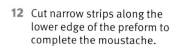

13 Place the moustache on the face. Use a tomato for the nose.

14 Cut off a side slice from a red grape.

15 Cut the slice in half. These are the eyelids.

16 Cut the leaves of the gooseberry in two. Arrange these around the head in the form of hair.

17 Cut the second strip of peel in two. These are the arms. Bend the tips. These are the hands.

18 Use a big red grape for the body. Attach the arms.

19 Cut half of a red grape into lengthwise quarters. These are the legs.

20 Attach the legs to the body. Use two pomegranate seeds for the boots.

Clown

INGREDIENTS

1 orange
1 mandarin
1 lime
1 green grape
1 red grape
1 strawberry
2 pomegranate seeds
blueberries

1 Cut off a side slice of the lime. The slice will be the chin. The rest is the face. Lay it cut side up.

2 Peel the mandarin and separate the segments. Place two segments under the face. These are the cheeks.

3 Place four segments on top. These make the forehead.

4 Place a segment below the face. Use two lime rounds for the ears.

5 Cut a crescent in the chin to make the mouth.

6 Cut teeth. Place the chin below the face.

7 Cut off the tips from the green grape. Cut the remaining middle piece into two round slices, without fully severing the two pieces. Unfold the rounds. These are the eyes.

8 Cut one grape tip in half. These are the eyelids.

9 Cut a side slice from the blueberry. Cut the slice in half. These are the pupils.

10 Cut a red grape in half lengthwise. Cut into quarters. These will be the eyebrows.

11 Lay the eyes on the face. Lay the eyelids above the eyes. Lay the pupils on the eyes.

12 Cut the strawberry in half to make the nose.

13 Place the nose and eyebrows on the face as shown.

14 Lay out blueberries in the form of a wig.

15 Cut a strip from an orange peel. Make incisions in it. This is the collar.

16 Lay the collar under the head.

17 Cut an orange into four segments.

18 Cut the peel off two of the segments. Cut one peel in half. These are the legs.

19 Cut the peel off another segment. Cut it in half. This is the body.

20 Lay out the body and legs. Use two strips of peel for the arms and two pomegranate seeds for the hands. Use quarters of red grape for boots.

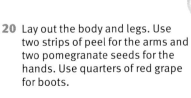

Lamb

INGREDIENTS

1 orange

2 round slices of lime

5 mandarin segments

1 green grape

2 red grapes

1 blue grape

1 Cut out some orange peel in the form of a semicircle. Insert a mandarin segment underneath. This makes the head.

2 Lay the orange on its base. This is the body and head.

3 Cut the red grapes in half.

4 Place the halves cut sides down. These are the hooves.

5 Lay the remaining mandarin segments between the body and hooves. These are the legs.

6 Make an incision in the peel of a lime slice.

7 Separate the peel. Bend the strip in the form of a horn.

8 Make one more horn. Fasten the horns under the head.

9 Cut off the outside slices from the green grape.

10 Cut the remaining middle piece in two. These are the eyes.

11 Cut two round slices from the blue grape. These are the pupils.

12 Place the pupils on the eyes. Place the eyes on the head.

Dog

INGREDIENTS

2 oranges
2 mandarins
1 lime
1 green grape
1 red grape
1 blue grape
1 blueberry

1 Cut semicircle flaps symmetrically on the each side of one orange. Lift the flaps and insert a mandarin segment underneath. This is the head with ears.

2 Cut a crescent of peel from the other mandarin. This is the muzzle and mouth.

3 Cut one round slice of orange in half. Separate the strips of peel.

4 Cut one strip into pieces. These are the teeth. Insert the teeth into the mouth under the peel.

5 Lay the muzzle against the head with a mandarin segment between to make the neck.

6 Cut out segments from green grape halves. These are the eyes.

7 Cut off two tips from the blueberry. These are the pupils.

8 Place the pupils on the eyes. Place the eyes on the head.

9 Use half of the blue grape for the nose. Use a slice of the red grape for the tongue.

10 Use half of the second orange for the body. Make an incision in it for the tail.

11 Insert a crescent of peel into the incision. This is the tail.

12 Cut off a round slice of lime.

13 Cut this slice in half. These are the paws. Cut out legs from the lime peel.

Flower

INGREDIENTS

2 mandarins
1 outer slice of grapefruit
1 lime

1 Peel one mandarin.

2 Separate it into segments.

3 Lay out the mandarin segments as shown in the form of a flower.

4 Place the slice of grapefruit in the center of the flower.

5 Make an incision in the round slice of lime.

6 Separate the peel.

7 Place the strip under the flower. This is the stem.

8 Cut an small outer slice of lime.

9 Cut this in half. These are the leaves.

10 Place them next to the stem.

11 To make a flowerpot, cut an edge slice off the other mandarin. Lay the mandarin cut side down. Lay the edge slice cut side up on top.

Dragon

INGREDIENTS

2 grapefruits

1 lime

1 green grape

1 blue grape

2 mandarin segments

2 mint leaves

1 Cut a round slice from one grapefruit.

2 Make an incision in the center. Separate all of the segments.

3 Bend this detail into the form of a crest.

4 Cut two outside pieces from the second grapefruit. Then cut off round slices.

5 Place one round slice at the end of the crest. This is the muzzle. Place a larger slice on top. This is the head.

6 Cut two edge rounds from the lime. These will be the eyes.

7 Cut circles from the blue grape. These are the pupils.

8 Cut out circles of peel from the edge slices.

9 Lay the lemon circles cut side up, and the lime circles on top cut side down. Lay the pupils on top. These are the eyes.

10 Cut off two rounds from the green grape. These are the nostrils.

11 Place the nostrils on the muzzle. Use mandarin segments for the legs. Use the mint leaves for the wings.

Parrot

INGREDIENTS

1 lime
1 slice of grapefruit
2 mandarin segments
1 orange segment
1 strawberry
1 green grape
1 blueberry

1 Slice up the strawberry. Cut each slice in half. Lay out the crest using the halves.

2 Cut an end slice of the grapefruit. Place it on the crest. This is the head.

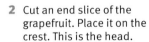

3 Cut an edge slice of lime.

4 Cut this slice in two. Lay out the beak.

5 Cut a slice of the green grape. Cut an edge round of the blueberry. These make the eye.

6 Place the eye on the head.

7 Use the orange segment for the body. Use the mandarin segments for the wings.

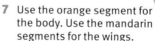

8 Cut out some mandarin peel in the form of a crescent. This is a feather.

9 Cut out a second feather from the mandarin peel. Cut out a third peel from the grapefruit peel.

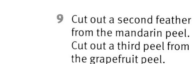

10 Lay out the tail from the feathers. Cut out two narrow strips from the mandarin peel. These are the legs.

11 Cut out feet from a red grape half as shown.

Bat

INGREDIENTS

2 round grapefruit slices
1 lime
2 mandarin segments
2 pomegranate seeds
1 strawberry
1 green grape

1 Cut a round slice from the grapefruit. Make an incision in the center. Separate all of the segments.

2 Bend this detail in the form of wings.

3 Cut off the tip of the lime.

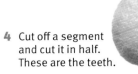

4 Cut off a segment and cut it in half. These are the teeth.

5 Place the teeth on the grapefruit slice. Use the remaining piece of lime slice for the muzzle. This is the head.

6 Cut the tips off the green grape. Cut the remaining middle piece into two rounds. These are the eyes.

7 Place the eyes on the head. Use the pomegranate seeds for the pupils.

8 Place the head on top of the wings.

9 Quarter the strawberry and arrange two pieces under the head. These are the ears. Use orange segments for the legs.

Flower 2

1 mandarin
1 lime
1 strawberry
blueberries

1 Make an incision in the center of the mandarin.

2 Make two more incisions, holding the knife at an angle. These are the tips of the petals.

3 Cut out petals, leaving the peel at the base of the mandarin uncut. Separate the petals from the mandarin.

4 Remove the mandarin.

5 Cut out teeth along the edges of the petals.

6 This is the flower.

7 Cut a lime in half.

8 Cut each half into three segments.

9 Separate the peel.

10 These are leaves. Place the leaves between the petals.

11 Cut off the base of a strawberry.

12 Place the strawberry in the center of the flower. Lay out blueberries in the form of a stem.

13 Cut a round slice from the lime.

14 Cut the slice in half. These are leaves. Attach the leaves to the stem.

Octopus

INGREDIENTS

1 mandarin

1 orange

1 green grape

2 pomegranate seeds

1 Cut a pointed strip of peel from the mandarin. This is a tentacle.

2 Cut out three more tentacles.

3 Cut out four tentacles on the other side symmetrically.

4 Turn the mandarin upside down.

5 Cut the orange in half. One half is the head.

6 Make a horizontal incision in the head. This is the mouth.

7 Cut out two pieces of orange peel from the other half. These are the teeth.

8 Insert the teeth in the mouth. Place the head on the tentacles.

9 Cut the green grape in half, without fully severing the two halves.

10 Unfold the halves. These are the eyes. Cut out segments to hold the pupils.

11 Place the eyes on the head.

12 Use pomegranate seeds for the pupils.

Rabbit

INGREDIENTS

1 orange

2 mandarin segments

1 round slice of grapefruit

1 green grape

1 blue grape

1 red grape

1 Cut the orange in half. One half is the head.

2 Make a horizontal incision in the head. This is the mouth.

3 Cut out two pieces of peel in the form of ears in the top of the head.

4 Bend up the ears. Cut out two pieces of orange peel. These are the teeth. Insert the teeth into the mouth.

5 Cut off a tip from the blue grape.

6 Cut the tip in half. These are the eyes.

7 Cut off a tip from the green grape. Cut this tip in half. These are the eyelids.

8 Join the eyes and eyelids. Place them in the openings under the ears.

9 Cut off a strip from a grapefruit semicircle. Cut it in half. These are the arms.

10 Place the arms on the second half of the orange. This is the body.

11 Cut a red grape in half lengthwise. These are the paws.

12 Attach the paws to the body. Use mandarin segments for the legs.

Exotic flower

INGREDIENTS

1 orange

1 lime

pomegranate seeds

1 Cut the orange peel in the form of a semicircle without severing it. This is a petal.

2 Cut a second petal on the opposite side symmetrically.

3 Cut two more petals as shown. Place the preform on its base.

4 Cut the peel between the petals from the base to the tip as shown.

5 Remove the pieces of peel.

6 Cut off the top half of the orange.

7 Bend and tuck the peel pieces, skin side up, under the orange.

8 Cut a segment from the lime. Separate the peel. This is the leaf.

9 Cut teeth at the edge of the leaf.

10 Make three more leaves. Place them between the petals.

11 Decorate the center of the flower with pomegranate seeds.

Melancholy Lion

INGREDIENTS

1 mandarin
1 grapefruit
2 green grapes
2 red grapes
2 pomegranate seeds

1 Cut out a pointed strip of mandarin peel and bend it outwards.

2 Cut similar strips around the mandarin.

3 This is the head.

4 Cut a red grape in half. These are the ears.

5 Place the ears under the head.

6 Cut halves from different-sized green grapes. These are the eyes. Use grape seeds for the pupils.

7 Insert the pupils into the eyes. Place the eyes on the head.

8 Cut off an outside slice of grapefruit. This is the muzzle.

9 Make an incision in the muzzle. This is the mouth.

10 Attach the muzzle to the head. Use a red grape for the nose.

11 Cut off a round slice of grapefruit. This is the body.

12 Cut out a tail from grapefruit peel.

13 Attach the body to the head. Cut out legs from mandarin peel. Attach the legs and tail to the body. Use pomegranate seeds for the paws.

Donkey

INGREDIENTS

1 orange

1 lime

1 grapefruit

1 mandarin segment

2 green grapes

2 blue grapes

1 Cut an orange in half. One half is the head. Make a horizontal incision.

2 Cut out two strips for the ears. Bend the ears up.

3 Cut a round slice of lime in two, without fully severing the two halves. These are the eyes.

4 Cut off two round slices from a blue grape. These are the pupils.

5 Cut a green grape in half. Cut one half into quarters. These are the eyelids.

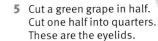

6 Place the pupils on the eyes. Place the eyelids on top. Place the eyes on the head.

7 Cut the grapefruit into round slices.

8 Insert the first grapefruit slice into the incision. This is the muzzle. Insert one more slice under the first one. This is the mouth.

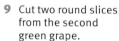

9 Cut two round slices from the second green grape.

10 Place these on the muzzle. These are the nostrils.

11 Attach the mandarin segment to the head. This is the neck. Use half of the lime for the body.

12 Cut off the peel from half of a grapefruit slice.

13 Cut the peel in two. These are the legs. Use a strip of lime peel for the tail.

14 Cut the tip off the second blue grape. Cut the tip in half. These are the hooves.

15 Attach the hooves to the legs.

Ladybug

INGREDIENTS

1 grapefruit

1 lime

1 green grape

1 blue grape

6 pomegranate seeds

1 Slice up the grapefruit.

2 Cut the biggest slice in half, without fully severing the two halves. These are the wings. Make tiny holes with a knife. Insert pomegranate seeds in the holes.

3 These are the wings.

4 Cut one more grapefruit slice in half. Cut off the strips of peel.

5 Cut each strip into three parts. These are the legs.

6 Lay out the legs. Place a grapefruit end slice on top. This is the body.

7 Place the wings on the body.

8 Cut half of the lime. This is the head.

9 Place the head against the body.

10 Cut two round slices from the green grape. These are the eyes.

11 Cut two round outer slices from the blue grape. These are the pupils.

12 Place the pupils on the eyes. Place the eyes on the head.

13 Use a thin strip of lime peel for the antennae.

Flower Pattern

1 Cut a flower on the grapefruit tip. Cut out a thin strip of peel along the contour.

2 Cut out a narrow section between the petals.

3 Cut the leaves and cut out a thin strip of peel along them.

4 Cut teeth around the edges of each leaf.

5 Cut out the sections around each tooth.

6 Cut out a leaf at the base of the grapefruit. Cut out a thin strip of peel along the contour.

7 Cut teeth along the edges of each leaf.

8 Cut veins on each.

9 Cut out the sections opposite each tooth. Cut leaves around the grapefruit.

10 Cut a lime in half.

11 Cut each half into three segments. Separate the peel. These are the leaves.

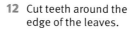

12 Cut teeth around the edge of the leaves.

13 Place the leaves around the grapefruit. Make similar leaves from the mandarin peel.

Hippo

INGREDIENTS

2 limes

1 green lemon (or another lime)

3 green grapes, 2 with stems

1 blue grape

1 One lime is the muzzle. Make an incision. This is the mouth. Make two semicircle cuts.

2 Bend the cut peel. These are the nostrils.

3 Cut the second lime in half.

4 One half is the head. Place it on the muzzle.

5 Cut two round slices from the blue grape. These are the pupils.

6 Cut one small hole in each of the stemmed green grapes. Insert the pupils. These are the eyes.

7 Cut the third green grape in half. These are the ears.

8 Place the eyes on the head. Place the ears under the head. Use the lemon for the body.

9 Cut a round slice from the remaining lime.

10 Cut the slice in half. These are the legs.

11 Place the legs under the body. Cut a narrow strip of lime peel. This is the tail.

12 It is also possible to make the hippo from an orange or a grapefruit.

Man 2

INGREDIENTS

1 orange
1 lime
2 green grapes
1 red grape
1 blueberry
2 blackberries
2 pomegranate seeds
1 cherry tomato

1 Cut an orange in half. One half will be the face.

2 Make two semicircle incisions. These are the eyelids. Cut out a mouth.

3 Bend the cut peel.

4 Cut half of a green grape into quarters. These are the eyes.

5 Cut a blueberry in half. These are the pupils.

6 Place the eyes under the eyelids. Place the pupils on the eyes.

7 Use two blackberries for the moustache. Use the tomato for the nose.

8 Cut a round end slice from the remaining orange half.

9 Place it under the face. This is the head.

10 Cut two round slices from the lime. Cut one slice in half. One half is a visor.

11 Place the visor on the forehead. Place another lime slice on top. This is the cap. Use green grape halves for the ears.

12 Cut a strip of lime peel for the arms. Use half of the lime for the body.

13 Cut a circle of orange peel in half. These are the legs.

14 Cut a red grape half into quarters. These are the boots.

15 Attach the legs and boots. Use two pomegranate seeds for the hands.

Palm tree

INGREDIENTS

1 orange

1 lime

1 cherry tomato

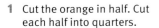

1 Cut the orange in half. Cut each half into quarters.

2 Cut all quarters into two segments.

3 Cut off a thin strip of the internal side of each segment.

4 Cut out the pulp.

5 Cut the peel into two triangles.

6 Make two more triangles.

7 Lay out the triangles in the form of the palm trunk.

8 Cut a lime in half.

9 Cut each half into three segments.

10 Separate the peel.

11 These are the palm leaves.

12 Cut teeth along the edges of each leaf.

13 Lay out the leaves.

14 Arrange the lime segments under the tree. Use the tomato for the sun.

Queen

INGREDIENTS

1 orange
1 lime
1 green grape
1 red grape
1 blueberry
9 blackberries
1 cherry tomato
2 pomegranate seeds

1 Cut an orange in half. One half is the head. Make two semicircle incisions for the eyelids. Cut out a mouth.

2 Bend the cut peel. This is the face.

3 Cut a green grape half into quarters. These are the eyes.

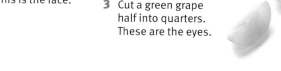

4 Cut a blueberry in half. These are the pupils.

5 Place the eyes under the eyelids. Place the pupils on the eyes.

6 Use the tomato for the nose. Lay out the blackberries in the shape of hair.

7 Use half of the lime for the body. Cut a strip of peel from a slice of lime. These are the arms.

8 Cut a circle from orange peel. Cut this into three parts.

9 Attach the two side slices. Place the middle part on top. This is the skirt.

10 Use pomegranate seeds for the hands. Use narrow strips of orange peel for the legs.

11 Cut out a crown from grapefruit peel.

12 Cut the red grape in half. Cut out shoes from the halves.

Lovely Flower

INGREDIENTS

1 mandarin

1 round slice of lime

6 mint leaves

1 Cut out peel in the center of the mandarin in the form of a flower.

2 Cut out leaves between the petals.

3 Cut peel between petals from the center of flower to the tip of the leaves.

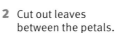

4 Separate the cut strips of peel.

5 Bend them under the mandarin.

6 Separate the petals from the mandarin.

7 Place the round slice of lime in the center of the flower.

8 Decorate with mint leaves.

Duck

1 Use the two lemons for the body and head.

2 Cut two segments from the orange.

3 Cut out the pulp.

4 The two pieces of peel are the beak.

5 Place the beak on the head.

6 Cut the green grape in half, without fully severing. Unfold the halves. These are the eyes.

7 Cut the blueberry in half. These are the pupils.

8 Place the pupils on the eyes. Place the eyes on the head.

9 Cut a slice from the lime. This is the wing.

10 Cut out plumage.

11 Cut one more orange segment. Cut out peel and cut it into two triangular pieces. These are the feet.

12 Cut out toes.

13 Place the wing on the body and place the feet under the body.

Pig

INGREDIENTS

2 oranges

1 green grape

1 red grape

1 blue grape

1 Cut an orange in half. Cut one half into quarters.

2 Cut the quarters into two segments.

3 Cut out the pulp. Cut the peel into triangles. These are the legs.

4 Arrange the legs. Place the other half of the orange on top. This is the body.

5 Bend a narrow strip of peel into the form of a tail.

6 Cut the second orange in half.

7 Place one half on the body. This is the head. Lay the tail next to the body.

8 Cut out a circle of orange peel. Cut this in two. These are the ears.

9 Cut two round slices from a blue grape. These are the eyes.

10 Place the eyes on the head. Place the ears under the head.

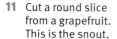

11 Cut a round slice from a grapefruit. This is the snout.

12 Cut two round slices of the green grape for the nostrils. Cut out a segment from the red grape for the mouth.

13 Place the nostrils and mouth on the snout. Place the snout on the head.

Flower in Vase

INGREDIENTS

2 mandarins
pomegranate seeds
blueberries
2 mint leaves

1 Cut out the peel in the center of one mandarin in the form of a flower.

2 Cut out leaves between the petals.

3 Cut the peel between the petals from the center of the flower to the tip of the leaves.

4 Separate the cut strips of peel and leaves.

5 Separate the cut peel in one piece. This is the flower.

6 Bend the tips of the cut strips under the flower.

7 Place the pomegranate seeds in the center of the flower.

8 Lay out the stem from the blueberries. Put the mint leaves against it.

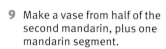

9 Make a vase from half of the second mandarin, plus one mandarin segment.

Flowerbed

INGREDIENTS

1 mandarin

2 red grapes

1 lime

peel of lemon or grapefruit

3 blueberries

1 strawberry

4 green grapes

1 Cut out a flower from the mandarin peel.

2 Separate the flower. Put a round slice of red grape into the center of the flower.

3 Lay out a flowerbed using round slices of lime.

4 Make a lot of flowers and lay them on the flowerbed.

5 Cut a round slice of grapefruit peel. Make small cuts around the slice.

6 Cut out the peel at an angle to make petals.

7 Make six similar flowers. Lay them on the flowerbed.

8 Cut off the outside slices from a strawberry.

9 Cut the middle part of the strawberry in two.

10 These are butterfly wings.

11 Use a lengthwise quarter of a red grape for the body. Use a blueberry for the head. Use thin strips of mandarin peel for the antennae.

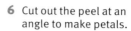

12 Cut a green grape in half without fully severing. Unfold the halves. These are wings for another butterfly. Make two more wings. Lay out similar body, head and antennae.

Poodle

INGREDIENTS

1 mandarin
1 grapefruit
1 green grape
1 red grape
1 blueberry

1 Peel the mandarin. Separate the segments.

2 One segment is the head.

3 Arrange two segments symmetrically, with their straight edges facing each other. This is the mouth.

4 Peel the grapefruit. Separate the segments. Remove the membranes.

5 Put two grapefruit segments against the head. These are the ears.

6 Cut off the tips from the green grape. Cut the remaining middle part in half, without fully severing. Unfold the halves. These are the eyes.

7 Cut two outside slices from the blueberry. These are the pupils.

8 Place the pupils on the eyes. Place the eyes on the head.

9 Cut half of the red grape. This is the nose.

10 Place the nose on the muzzle.

11 Cut a round slice of grapefruit in half. Cut off the strips of peel.

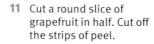

12 One of the strips is the neck. Cut the other strip in two. These are the legs. Use two grapefruit segments for the body and tail.

13 Place the legs under the body. Use small pieces of grapefruit segment for the paws.

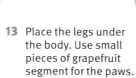

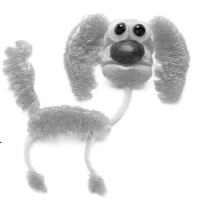

Walking Sun

1 orange

1 orange segment

1 red grape

1 green grape

1 blueberry

1 Cut a circular slice of orange peel. Cut the remaining orange into rounds.

2 Select the biggest round. Cut the peel and separate the segments.

3 Cut out small triangular sections of peel between the segments.

4 Bend the preform into the form of a ring. These are sun beams.

5 Place another orange slice on top.

6 Cover with the circular slice of orange peel. This is the sun.

7 Cut off the tips from the green grape. Cut the remaining middle piece in half, without fully severing. Unfold the halves. These are the eyes.

8 Cut two outer slices from the blueberry. These are the pupils.

9 Place the pupils on the eyes. Place the eyes on the sun.

10 Cut out a strip of peel.

11 Cut a piece of strip for the mouth.

12 Arrange the orange segment for the body. The pieces of the strip of peel are the legs and arms.

13 Cut half of the red grape into quarters. These are the boots.

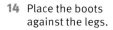

14 Place the boots against the legs.

Horse

INGREDIENTS

1 orange

1 grapefruit slice

1 lime

1 red grape

1 green grape

1 blue grape

1 blueberry

1 Cut a strip of orange peel. Make a narrow incision. This is the mane.

2 Cut an oval from the grapefruit peel. This is the head.

3 Cut half of the red grape into quarters. These are the ears.

4 Arrange the head, ears and mane.

5 Cut off the tips from the green grape. Cut one tip in half. These are the eyelids. Cut the remaining middle piece in half, without fully severing. Unfold the halves. These are the eyes.

6 Cut off an outer slice from the blueberry. Cut the slice in half. These are the pupils.

7 Place the pupils and eyelids on the eyes. Place the eyes on the head.

8 Cut off an outer slice from the lime. This is the muzzle. Cut out some peel in the form of a crescent. This is the mouth.

9 Cut out teeth. Place the muzzle on the head.

10 Cut half of the orange into four segments.

11 Cut out the pulp from two segments. Cut one piece of peel in two. These are the legs.

12 Cut out a triangle from the second piece of peel. Make incisions in it. This is the tail.

13 Cut half of the blue grape into quarters. These are the hooves.

14 Use half of the orange for the body. Place the legs and tail under the body. Add hooves.

Pirate

INGREDIENTS

1 orange

2 mandarin segments

1 lime

1 red grape

2 green grapes

1 blue grape

1 strawberry

1 blueberry

2 pomegranate seeds

1 Cut a strip of orange peel. Make narrow incisions in it. This is the beard.

2 One slice of orange is the head.

3 Place the beard on the head. Add the two mandarin segments. Use two grape slices for the ears.

4 Cut the tips from the green grape. The remaining middle piece is an ear.

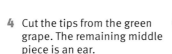

5 Cut half of a blueberry slice. This is the pupil. Cut half from the tip of a green grape for an eyelid.

6 Cut a slice of blue grape. This is an eye patch.

7 Place the pupil and eyelid on the eye. Place the eye on the head.

8 Place half of the strawberry on the face. This is the nose. Use half of the lime for the body.

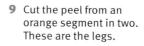

9 Cut the peel from an orange segment in two. These are the legs.

10 Cut a segment from a slice of lime. This is a wooden leg.

11 Cut two strips of orange peel. These are the arms.

12 Use pomegranate seeds for the hands. Use quarters of red grape for the boot.

13 Cut a segment from an orange slice. This is the hat. Decorate with strips of lime peel and red grape slices.

Old Man

INGREDIENTS

1 orange

3 mandarin segments

1 lime

2 green grapes

1 red grape

1 blueberry

2 pomegranate seeds

1 One slice of orange is the head. Use two slices of lime for the ears.

2 Cut out a strip of the orange peel. Make narrow incisions in it. This is the hair.

3 Place the hair on the head.

4 Cut the tips from a green grape. These are the eyes.

5 Cut one tip from the second grape in half. These are the eyelids.

6 Cut an outer slice from the blueberry in half. These are the pupils.

7 Place the pupils and eyelids on the eyes. Place the eyes on the head. Use quarters of red grape for the eyebrows.

8 Place one mandarin segment between the eyes. This is the nose. Place another segment under the nose.

9 Use quarters of red grape for the moustache. Place one more mandarin segment under the first segment. This is the chin.

10 Cut off an outer slice of lime. Cut out peel in the form of a crescent. This is the mouth.

11 Cut teeth. Place the mouth on the chin.

12 Cut thin strips of orange peel. These are the arms and legs.

13 Use one orange segment for the body. Place the legs and arms against the body. Use the pomegranate seeds for the boots.

A FIREFLY BOOK

Published by Firefly Books Ltd. 2017

First printing

PUBLISHER CATALOGING-IN-PUBLICATION DATA (U.S.)
A CIP record for this title is available from Library of Congress

LIBRARY AND ARCHIVES CANADA CATALOGUING IN PUBLICATION
A CIP record for this title is available from Library and Archives Canada

Published in the United States by
Firefly Books (U.S.) Inc.
P.O. Box 1338, Ellicott Station
Buffalo, New York 14205

Published in Canada by
Firefly Books Ltd.
50 Staples Avenue, Unit 1
Richmond Hill, Ontario L4B 0A7

Cover and interior design: Peter Ross / Counterpunch Inc.

Printed in China

We acknowledge the financial support of the Government of Canada.

MIX
Paper from
responsible sources
FSC
www.fsc.org   FSC® C016973